Interactive Press
Beerstorming with Charlotte Brontë in New York

Rachel J Fenton lives in Oamaru in Te Waipounamu, Aotearoa, where she is Curator of Janet Frame House. Winner of the NZSA Laura Solomon Cuba Press Prize 2022 for her partially graphic novel *Between the Flags*, she placed second in the 2014 Dundee International Book Prize for *Some Things the English* and also won the Auckland University of Technology Graphic Fiction Prize. AKA Rae Joyce, she co-edited *Three Words, An Anthology of Aotearoa Women's Comics* (Beatnik, 2015) and was awarded a Creative New Zealand Arts Grant to research and write a graphic biography of Mary Taylor, the best friend of Charlotte Brontë.

Interactive Press
Brisbane

T0359606

Beerstorming with Charlotte Brontë in New York

Rachel J. Fenton

Interactive Press
an imprint of IP (Interactive Publications Pty Ltd)
Treetop Studio • 9 Kuhler Court
Carindale, Queensland, Australia 4152
sales@ipoz.biz
http://ipoz.biz/shop

Printed in 16 pt Avenir on 12 pt Adobe Caslon Pro.

ISBN: 978192830838 (PB); 978192830845 (eBk)

for Sylvia Petter and Lori Tiron-Pandit, in friendship

Contents

Beerstorming

verb

The practice of upgrading regular brainstorming sessions to include your favorite craft beer. Beerstorming sessions result in improved cooperation, creativity, and morale almost 100 percent of the time.
– https://beerandbrewing.com/beerslanging/

New York

New York, cold as discovery
on the Friday morning my mother's text
informs me my father had a heart
attack – we are estranged;
what is to be done about that?

Not one, two, but three four five

days of visiting libraries
I can leave but never recover
from. Charlotte's waiting. Truth

> will   be cradled
> spine felt
> green   as a cover
> against a wall

> of books, one I'll return to

in photographs, blurred as froth on beer
pulled too fast from the tap.

New York Public Library

Friday, later: paper, thin,
blue as the New York sky
missing a piece of brown

high rise. I pause opposite
gold doors of Gotham Hall,

buy two tall hot teas,
take off my gloves,
check the temperature,

> weather report.
> Minus five.

At the place I thought I wanted,
impatient attendants inform
me: the one you want is over

the road. Guarded by a white lion
expression in stone, staunch
Leo. Inside it's a palace.

The Berg Collection

A man roars at the end of a red corridor.
Charlotte comes in snatched moments,
words time has made mud in water.
Joshua is good at pretending he hasn't heard.

Tonight, we will share ideas, beers
bought with a bottle opener from a drug store

on a corner where streets
whose names and numbers
I struggle to remember
meet.

For months, they have prepared, brought gifts.
Tin tin tin. They have been watching Happy Valley.

But first, Joshua repeats instructions
for what to bring to the table, leave
in the cloakroom where women
do not speak regardless of how much I smile.

It's cold where they work beside the revolving
door, hard to push

as it is. All Saturday I pour, luckily
miss the manuscript
I am allowed to touch
with hands that did this:

Martha died. "There is nothing to regret"
I confide in Joshua, the coat check guy is jolly
grumpy. He laughs

librarianly. An engineer is told
humidity is threatening the safety of the collection.

Curator of the Berg Collection

Even though he has sharpened my Blackwing,
Joshua has given me a red pencil
inscribed with New York Public Library in gold,
with four sheets of yellow
paper. The thinness pleases
me as much as a five-hundred-gram block of sunshine
spread like a pyramid's angular shaft
on its side next to Mary's comparable leaf
would, though hers is blue.

I have dragged the end of Auckland
summer into New York's winter. Grey,
pushing in front of me, notes on every line read.

Referencing the Collection

Charlotte, how do you feel, here
among the brownstones instead

of Helstones? That "lump of perfection",
Rose York? What can be said in longhand

next to your rushed slant? Cursively,
we are not alike, as Martha to Mary

Taylor. Not sisters but friends,
merely miles by moorland in one respect

though continents, nay worlds
apart where we will end.

About the Collection

But for small details, such as how no two are the same
(though, do we know with certainty?) this day will end
as it began;

but for getting lost, for two hours in a grid I cannot read,
long streets people mistake for privacy (yes, what is said
about New Yorkers);

but for it being too cold to snow, following a tall man in,
turning, ignoring another's *do you want a table, darling?*
collar up again;

but for cold dark ale, mopping hot creamy lobster bisque
with sweet soft bread (Irish keep I couldn't work out a tip
for), basketball;

but for this city, lights everywhere except my hotel room,
WhatsApp call out of my timezone, *How are you feeling,
today?* A snowflake.

Access to the Collection

Charlotte sends me a WhatsApp: *We're only up,*
not dressed and ready just yet. At eight-thirty am
New York City is not open for breakfast on Sunday.
New Yorkers are in bed watching CNN in-between
commercials praising Donald Trump for
Making America Great Again. We walk three blocks
then turn back to eat at the place opposite our hotel.
Charlotte lets me buy breakfast. She did not
lose her baby.

Fifth Avenue

Charlotte's baby wants always to be carried,
calls me *tanti*. He wears a backpack. In it, objects –
they go where he goes. Now and then he will unzip

to slowly check they are still where he put them. His
favourite activity is to count, thing after thing
until he reaches *Five*! Naming is not his priority.

Sesame Street

NYC, you are easy as navigating Sesame Street;
knowing it's here doesn't tell me how to get there.

In old York, shire signs have points
to
                                Mytholmes
                                Goose Cote
                                Moorside
                                Field Head
                                Dimples

– all lanes

      Lee, Sun, Hob Cote – same; names
teach me history,   not maths

whose symbols are anathema to me.
Your may-as-well-be-from-Mars

signs are as coded as price tags.
Who can remember the cost of each village?

Who can't forget Lumberfoot and Grey Scar
roads? I reckon fair-to-middling, like

Wide Lane   standing
Slack Lane   on toes at the dance,
Green   the fight afterwards.
Gill
Grange
Harehills, Oldfield, Back Lane – these lanes
love me Big Bird obviously. Why not you?

Comparison is a form of self-abuse,
according to Oprah Winfrey. Vis-à-vis;

they call you New York, but all you've done is
exchange my names for a blizzard of numbers.

Brooklyn Bridge

Snowstorms are forecast.

One week earlier:
irony is a white business man in Chicago
holding a brown card declaring in black Vivid:
Muslims Welcome, *This Land is Your Land.*

Women have organised protests. I walk behind
a pigeon with one foot I've seen in every city
I've been. Waiting

on the sidewalk for a cab that isn't yellow or Uber,
names compact. Snow shovelled to the sides
remains intact in the shade
blackened by pollution. Only now I see one,
I see many.

The fall was heavy, then.

Charlotte's husband speaks several languages
until he hits upon pidgin the driver and he share
between Mumbai and Kolkata. They talk

the whole way to the Museum of the Native American
Indian. Charlotte feels uneasy about crossed swords
charming the rear-view mirror. Her husband's family
prize pale skin. East River foils
the law of simultaneous contrast

eternally. I fail
to stymie tears when saying goodbye, I turn to the lift
from holding Charlotte's son to where mine should be.

February again.

Reprographic Orders

Charlotte is not herself today, but she is my friend.
She laughs Ludicrously beautifully, pats her hand
on my knee as if we have grown up in the same town
though we are meeting for the first time.
She allows me to play aeroplanes with her son.
In my arms, he is as light as a ghost, and as heavy
in my mind. He calls, Again, again, tanti,
and interprets Cooper Hewitt as Super Cutie,
which is him. There are two versions of the world
and everything in his is sunny days.

Only afterwards, when alone in a hotel room that looks
out onto broken heart script of fire escapes, discarded
syringes, where last night I heard screaming
and this morning men's
voices accompanying a knock on my grey window,
I look up the meaning of his name
for me. Tanti means auntie in Romanian,
his mother's tongue. In his father's Hindi,
it refers to one of a tribe of weavers,
of the Dalits, formerly discriminated against in India
as "most backward classes"[1] and I wonder,
who he will take after.

---

[1]   http://www.catchnews.com/india-news/eyes-wide-shut-dalit-votes-welcome-in-bihar-not-their-woes-1440265325.html

Doing the Morgan

My escort is called Security, for the purpose of taking
me from the nook where my entry is observed
to the glass lift I suppose I should call my elevator.
Only he can make it work.
A key on his belt is inserted above the numbers
and he presses. It goes up. It stops
on the highest level. He pushes
double doors open. Then I'm left
to wash my hands and touch
manuscripts overlooked by rarer books.

Sherman Fairchild Reading Room

All kinds of theft
present to me
when I observe
rare books behind
glass balconies:

book thieves are least
of these. The words
you took and told
to someone else
as if your own

to give, impress,
undress, were mine.
An aperture.
I'm betrayed by
my thoughts, my mind.

Permission to Take Photographs

Hours from now I will pin-point the difference between
undulate and pivotal when referring to tassels twisted from
lucky threads to titillate six or five old men while a woman
takes pictures with her phone for her husband who has
his back to the stage. He is turning red. A jazz band plays
old time hits making much of a trombone. Lederhosen-
wearing wait-staff compete for our service. My friend knows
the barkeep and introduces me. I say: You look like my
grandfather, when he was alive, obviously. My friend decants
a pitcher into the two large glasses we have drained. It's my
fault. I had instructed: tea, food, beer, in that order. We are
here via a French café and Korea Town. The burlesque dancer
has beautiful breasts, has never fed children; her nipples will
respond to giving the way a stoic hardens to loss. Of course,
I would say that after a tankard and a half in Bierhaus NYC.
But this is Monday morning. I am in The Morgan and I have
permission to take photographs of Mary Taylor's letters to
her best friend Charlotte Brontë. The only stipulation, I must
sign, they are for my private research use, must not be shared.
The Berg has its own rules.

Revisiting the Berg

only now I realise the corridor is lined
with illustrations   some duplicates
everyone black and white

                    photographs remind me
                    I can go back   re-read
                    but never unknow

Last Poem in NYC

The only living boy in New York caught the evening
Train from Penn Station back home with his mom,

dad and big sister, but as is typical of narratives
in our generation, sisters rarely get a mention.

So, here's to the girl, sassy and chill, still and cool
when all about is his, he, him. Here's to her refusal

to please, to talk, insistently wearing earphones
in restaurants and hotel rooms,

stiff-shouldering attempts to curry favour, be auntie –
why should she embrace a woman she's never met?

Here's to her honesty, defiance that states its protest
despite shyness. She knows where she's heading

already. I've given her a small bowl, hand-formed
from a lump of New Zealand. Under thin blue glaze,

a spiral visible. I tilted for her, swallowed half a whale,
watched the rest swirl round the plughole in reverse.

J F K

I. New Yorkshire

doorman's missing teeth
church aisle between seats

two finger whistle hails a pew
twenty bucks for a favour

what difference does it make?
cabbie demands payment

via a clip on his phone instead of meter
a picture   fiancé?

I'm tired   I'm not happy
&   I'm getting out of car

II. Beatnik, Found Poem

██████ *I know how [inaudible] he is to this company*
but how can he do what he's doing to you?
Don't you realise
there is a difference?   *It's sick. It's sick.*
Believe me   *both of them. I know.*
I know. I know. It's a disgr. I know.
*When I'm back from Israel. Who knows. *Blows kiss**

III. Gate ■

Could you pencil me in.
The twenty-fourth would be wonderful
but for it being my birthday.

I can't stop transcribing, can't shut off
the lines. I've read
text like a tapestry

Seahorse Ranch [underlined]
Underneath I transcribe:
solo energy & global energy
I'd like to pick your brains
brainstorm with you. Charlotte Brontë
has left me her bottle opener, WhatsApps:
Already it's snowing in Maine.

Research Findings

At the point where five black lines meet
between five grey flagstones, a blue note,
folded to obscure all but fragments of the words *strip,*
fresh gin, is dropped in Chicago
five days before my research begins in NYC.
I took a photograph, a shifting of tense, proof,
it was all mapped out on the sidewalk; what's to come,
a moment in the past's revealing.

Acknowledgements

My thanks to Sara Lefsyk, without whom this collection would not have gotten out of the archive. Thanks also to the editors of the following journals in which some of these poems first appeared: "About the Collection" and "Brooklyn Bridge" were published in *English, Journal of the English Association* (Oxford Academic), Volume 66, Issue 255; "Permission to Take Photographs" was published in *Landfall* Issue 234 (Otago University Press); "New York" first appeared in *Ethel Zine*. Thanks, too, go to Lori, for friendship and inspiration.

Manufactured by Amazon.com.au
Sydney, New South Wales, Australia

18420833R00020